Influential Presidents
John F. Kennedy

by Emma Huddleston

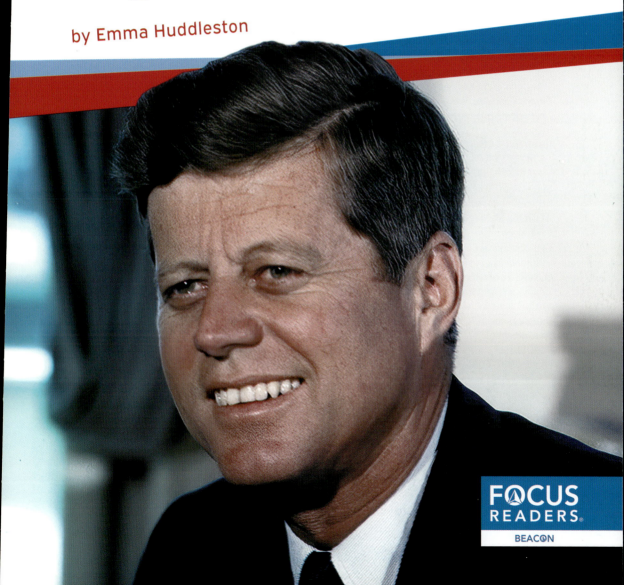

FOCUS READERS®
BEACON

www.focusreaders.com

Copyright © 2023 by Focus Readers®, Lake Elmo, MN 55042. All rights reserved. No part of this book may be reproduced or utilized in any form or by any means without written permission from the publisher.

Focus Readers is distributed by North Star Editions:
sales@northstareditions.com | 888-417-0195

Produced for Focus Readers by Red Line Editorial.

Photographs ©: Cecil Stoughton/National Archives/Wikimedia, cover, 1; AP Images, 4, 6, 12, 14, 17, 20–21, 25, 29; Boston Globe/AP Images, 8; Nelly George/Alamy, 11; Horst Faas/AP Images, 19; Niday Picture Library/Alamy, 22; Charles Tasnadi/AP Images, 27

Library of Congress Cataloging-in-Publication Data
Names: Huddleston, Emma, author.
Title: John F. Kennedy / by Emma Huddleston.
Description: Lake Elmo, MN : Focus Readers, [2023] | Series: Influential
    presidents | Includes bibliographical references and index. | Audience:
    Grades 2-3
Identifiers: LCCN 2022036165 (print) | LCCN 2022036166 (ebook) | ISBN
    9781637394649 (hardcover) | ISBN 9781637395011 (paperback) | ISBN
    9781637395721 (ebook pdf) | ISBN 9781637395387 (hosted ebook)
Subjects: LCSH: Kennedy, John F. (John Fitzgerald), 1917-1963--Juvenile
    literature. | Presidents--United States--Biography--Juvenile literature.
    | United States--Politics and government--1961-1963--Juvenile
    literature.
Classification: LCC E842.Z9 H84 2023 (print) | LCC E842.Z9 (ebook) | DDC
    973.922092 [B]--dc23/eng/20220802
LC record available at https://lccn.loc.gov/2022036165
LC ebook record available at https://lccn.loc.gov/2022036166

Printed in the United States of America
Mankato, MN
012023

About the Author

Emma Huddleston lives in Minnesota with her husband and daughter. She enjoys reading, writing, and staying active. She thinks learning about presidents is an important part of understanding how the United States works today.

Table of Contents

CHAPTER 1
A New Era 5

CHAPTER 2
Becoming a Leader 9

CHAPTER 3
Fighting Communism 15

ISSUE SPOTLIGHT
Cuban Missile Crisis 20

CHAPTER 4
Death of a President 23

Focus on John F. Kennedy • 28
Glossary • 30
To Learn More • 31
Index • 32

Chapter 1

A New Era

John F. Kennedy stepped onto a stage. A large crowd spread out before him. The date was January 20, 1961. Kennedy had just become president of the United States. It was time for his speech.

Kennedy delivers a speech after being sworn in as president.

 A crowd gathered outside the US Capitol to hear Kennedy's speech.

Kennedy spoke loudly and clearly. He promised to make big changes. Kennedy named four problems. He said war, **poverty**, disease, and **tyranny** were hurting people. Kennedy planned to fight these problems.

Kennedy wanted to bring peace and fairness to the world. He also wanted Americans to help their country. The crowd cheered. A new **era** in US history was beginning.

Kennedy was the youngest person to be elected president. He was 43 years old when he took office.

Chapter 2

Becoming a Leader

John F. Kennedy was born on May 29, 1917. He grew up in Massachusetts. When he finished high school, Kennedy went to Harvard University. He studied government and history.

John F. Kennedy played football when he was in high school.

After college, Kennedy joined the US Navy. He served in World War II (1939–1945). Kennedy was in charge of a small boat. His crew had 12 men. Their job was to stop Japanese supply ships.

In 1943, a Japanese ship sank Kennedy's boat. Kennedy hurt

Kennedy had three brothers and five sisters. His brothers also served in the military. The oldest, Joseph, died in World War II.

 Kennedy (far right) poses with his crew during World War II.

his back during the attack. But he still led his group. They swam to a nearby island. Then they were rescued.

 Kennedy meets with mill workers in 1958.

After the war, Kennedy started his career in government. In 1946, he became a US **representative** for Massachusetts. Six years later, he was elected to the US Senate. As a lawmaker, Kennedy pushed for higher pay for workers. He also tried to create more housing at lower prices.

Kennedy was very popular in Massachusetts. In 1958, he won a second **term** in the Senate. But he was planning to run for an even higher office.

When Kennedy was young, his family called him Jack. He kept this nickname as an adult.

Chapter 3

Fighting Communism

In 1960, John F. Kennedy ran for president. He said he would help businesses grow. He also wanted to help other countries, especially ones with new governments. By doing that, he hoped to gain **allies**.

Kennedy waves to supporters during the 1960 election.

Kennedy ran against Richard Nixon. The election was very close. Kennedy won a narrow victory.

As president, Kennedy often focused on Communism. Communism is an **economic** system. In this system, the government owns all property.

In 1960, Kennedy and Nixon took part in a **debate**. It was the first presidential debate shown on TV.

 Kennedy and Richard Nixon stand in a TV studio after their debate in 1960.

Kennedy wanted to stop Communism from spreading. He wanted to spread capitalism instead. In that system, individual people own property.

17

In 1961, Kennedy sent a group of fighters to Cuba. This country had a Communist government. Kennedy wanted to end Communism in Cuba. But Cuba's army stopped the invasion. It was a major failure.

Kennedy also continued the Vietnam War (1954–1975). In this war, the US military was fighting Communist forces. US troops were losing. But Kennedy did not want to accept defeat. So, he sent more soldiers to Vietnam.

 Thousands of Americans and millions of Vietnamese died during the Vietnam War.

Back home, Kennedy helped expand the US space program. He set a challenging goal. He wanted to send a person to the moon. Kennedy believed the United States could be the first country to do it.

ISSUE SPOTLIGHT

Cuban Missile Crisis

In 1962, the Soviet Union stored powerful bombs in Cuba. From Cuba, the bombs could reach the United States. Some people wanted Kennedy to attack the storage buildings in Cuba. But Kennedy thought that would make the problem worse. Instead, he ordered the US military to block Soviet ships that were traveling to Cuba. That way, the Soviet Union could not deliver more bombs. A few days later, Kennedy reached an agreement with the Soviet leader. The world had avoided a horrible war.

A US ship (front) inspects a Soviet ship near Cuba in November 1962.

Chapter 4

Death of a President

John F. Kennedy planned to run for a second term. He gave speeches. He spoke about world peace and helping the environment. On November 22, 1963, he went to Texas. His wife, Jackie, joined him.

Kennedy rides through Dallas, Texas, in November 1963.

They rode through the streets of Dallas in a parade.

Suddenly, gunshots rang out. Kennedy was shot in the head and neck. His driver quickly went to the nearest hospital. But it was too late. Kennedy was dead.

People around the world mourned Kennedy's death. Millions watched his funeral on TV.

Kennedy served a short time in office. But he left a huge **legacy**. People viewed him as a symbol

 Kennedy's wife and two young children mourn his death.

of hope. They remembered him for trying to solve difficult issues. For example, Kennedy pushed for **civil rights.**

In the early 1960s, many Black people could not vote. And they could not go to the same public places as white people. So, Kennedy asked Congress to pass new laws. Congress didn't do this when Kennedy was alive. But President Lyndon B. Johnson signed several civil rights laws in the 1960s.

Did You Know?

Lyndon B. Johnson became the new president after Kennedy was killed.

 Police officers carry away a protester during a 1965 civil rights march.

Kennedy's legacy grew in another way after his death. In 1969, US astronauts walked on the moon. They reached the goal that Kennedy had set in 1961.

FOCUS ON
John F. Kennedy

Write your answers on a separate piece of paper.

1. Write a paragraph describing Kennedy's career before he became president.

2. Do you think the United States should try to change the governments of other countries? Why or why not?

3. Where did Kennedy die?
   - **A.** Texas
   - **B.** Cuba
   - **C.** Vietnam

4. How did Kennedy affect civil rights?
   - **A.** As president, he signed many laws.
   - **B.** He asked Congress to pass new laws, which it did after he died.
   - **C.** He tried to stop Congress from passing civil rights laws.

5. What does **narrow** mean in this book?

*The election was very close. Kennedy won a **narrow** victory.*

    A. barely enough
    B. heavy or large
    C. bored and tired

6. What does **mourned** mean in this book?

*People around the world **mourned** Kennedy's death. Millions watched his funeral on TV.*

    A. didn't know about
    B. died suddenly
    C. showed sadness

Answer key on page 32.

Glossary

allies
Nations or people that are on the same side.

civil rights
Rights that protect people's freedom and equality.

debate
A discussion about different ways to deal with an issue.

economic
Having to do with the system of goods, services, money, and jobs in a certain place.

era
A period of history.

legacy
The things a person becomes known for.

poverty
Not having enough money or resources to live easily.

representative
A person who speaks on behalf of a larger group.

term
The amount of time a person can serve after being elected.

tyranny
When a government uses its power in a cruel way.

To Learn More

BOOKS

Gunderson, Megan M. *John F. Kennedy.* Minneapolis: Abdo Publishing, 2021.

Harper, Judith E. *John F. Kennedy.* Mankato, MN: The Child's World, 2020.

Moore, Shannon Baker. *John F. Kennedy's Assassination Rocks America.* Mankato, MN: The Child's World, 2018.

NOTE TO EDUCATORS

Visit **www.focusreaders.com** to find lesson plans, activities, links, and other resources related to this title.

Index

C
capitalism, 17
civil rights, 25–26
Communism, 16–18
Congress, 26
Cuba, 18, 20

D
debate, 16

J
Johnson, Lyndon B., 26

M
military, 10, 18, 20
moon, 19, 27

N
Nixon, Richard, 16

S
Soviet Union, 20
space program, 19

U
US Navy, 10
US representative, 12
US Senate, 12–13

V
Vietnam War, 18

W
World War II, 10

Answer Key: 1. Answers will vary; 2. Answers will vary; **3.** A; **4.** B; **5.** A; **6.** C